For Kevin, Laura, Curt, and Leah

With thanks to Katie Heit and Marietta Zacker
—D. Robbins

For all the powerful girls and women
—M. Joshi

Library of Congress Cataloging-in-Publication Data available

ISBN 978-1-338-89507-0 (PB) / 978-1-338-89508-7 (RLB)

10 9 8 7 6 5 4 3 2 1                    24 25 26 27 28

Printed in China    38

First edition, January 2024

Book design by Brian LaRossa

# YOU ARE A STAR,
# MALALA
# YOUSAFZAI

WRITTEN BY
**DEAN ROBBINS**

ILLUSTRATED BY
**MAITHILI JOSHI**

SCHOLASTIC PRESS ★ NEW YORK

Do you know what I liked about my home in Mingora, Pakistan?

Gazing at the snowcapped mountains.

Smelling the heavenly spices from my mother's kitchen.

Hearing my brothers play on our street.

"Hi, Khushal! Hi, Atal!"

"Hi, Malala!"

But do you know what I liked *best* about Mingora?

Going to school!

Everyone says I have the happiest family.

Maybe that's why I'm always smiling!

## A PRAYER ON THE WATER

My family did not have much money, but others in Mingora had even less. So I wrote out a prayer, asking for courage to help those in need. I tied it to a piece of wood, put a dandelion on top, and let it float into the swirling Swat River. Would my prayer be answered?

My school uniform was a shalwar kamiz: a dark blue top draped over comfortable pants.

I loved the way they looked with my black scarf and pink backpack!

In class, I sat near my friends Moniba and Malka and tried as hard as I could in every subject.

Math. Science. Public speaking.

School helped my imagination soar.

And in my part of Pakistan, girls needed all the help we could get.

On special occasions, women in my town painted beautiful designs on their hands with a dye called henna.

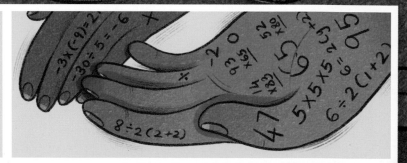

To show how much we valued learning, my friends and I painted ours differently—with math equations!

## EDUCATION FOR ALL

My father started our school because Mingora's girls rarely had a chance to learn. All were welcome, even the poorest children. If students came to class hungry, I invited them home for fried eggs, sugary tea, and delicious bread called chapati.

Every place has its own ways, and Mingora was no different.

Many people believed that men were more important than women and that boys were more important than girls.

My family did not agree!

Neither does Islam, the religion of my Muslim community.

Our school proved that girls could think for themselves and become anything they chose.

But it also angered a group of violent men called the Taliban.

How did I know that women were just as capable as men?

By watching my mother in action!

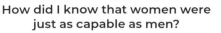

## MAKE WAY FOR GIRLS

My mother could not get an education, and neither could most of the girls from her village. When I was born, my father promised that life would be different for me. "If Malala only has a chance," he said, "she will move mountains!"

The Taliban hated everything I held dear.

Freedom. Equality. Education.

They swarmed into Mingora with their guns to demand that people follow their strict religious rules.

They even told girls not to go to school!

We had to stand up for our rights.

But how?

The Taliban stopped any girl carrying books because they knew she was on her way to school.

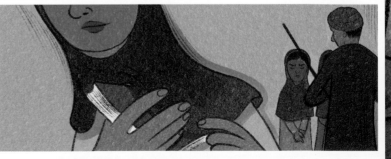

But I tricked them by hiding books under my shawl!

## WHAT TO DO?

When I see a problem, I always try to think of a solution. How could I stop the Taliban from ruining our lives? I daydreamed about waving a magic wand to make them disappear! But I knew I needed a plan that would really work.

With my family's help, I decided to oppose the Taliban peacefully.

I would defeat them with the power of ideas!

My father and I gave interviews on television and the radio.

"Save our schools," I said, "and save our Pakistan!"

The country's leader heard our plea.

The army arrived in Mingora to fight the Taliban, but that meant the rest of us had to flee to safety.

The Taliban actually tried to keep girls and women from laughing.

That was one rule I could *never* follow!

## FINDING MY VOICE

At first, I was shy about speaking out in public. But my confidence grew when I saw that my words could change minds. "Malala," my father told me, "your speeches go to the core of people's hearts." No one had ever seen an eleven-year-old girl defending her right to be in school!

People escaped Mingora in cars, trucks, buses, mule carts, and even wheelbarrows.

I wanted to take my books, but we had no room.

So I whispered a prayer to protect them from harm.

At last, we got to the faraway village of Shangla, where we slept on my uncle's dirt floor.

Would I ever see my home again?

My brother Atal wanted to take our chickens on the journey, but my parents told him they would poop in the car.

So he asked if we could put them in diapers!

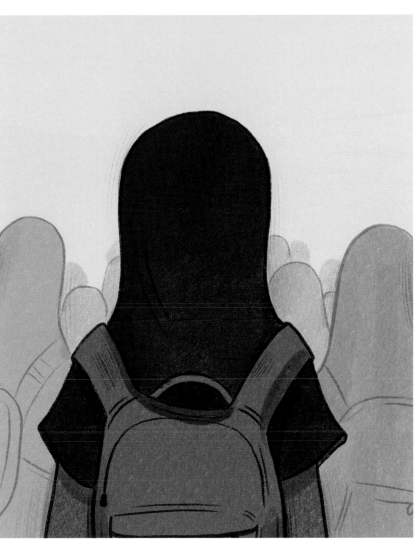

## MY OWN LITTLE PROTEST

In Shangla, we were called "displaced people" because violence had driven us from our home. But there was one good thing about being away from Mingora: I could go to school again without anyone trying to stop me! It felt like the best way to defy the Taliban.

When the army chased the Taliban out of Mingora, we returned to our house.

I was so happy to see the lovely Swat River for the first time in three months.

And you know what?

My books survived!

I picked each one up so I could say hello.

Soon, I returned to speaking about girls' education in front of even larger audiences.

Life got better in Mingora, at least for a little while.

My friends told me to dress up for a special event at school.

SURPRISE! It was a party to celebrate my success as an activist!

## THE MALALA SCHOOL

My message about education was spreading, and Pakistan even named a school after me. When I went for a visit, the students gave me a pretty painting. It showed me doing my favorite thing: dreaming!

Unfortunately, the Taliban crept back into town.

They threatened anyone who opposed them, even a fifteen-year-old girl like me.

I just ignored them and went to school every day.

But I did start taking the bus, which was safer than walking.

On October 9, 2012, Moniba and I sat next to each other on the bus ride home.

Someone stepped into the street and forced our bus to stop.

I have no memory of what happened next.

On that same October day, my mother prepared for lessons in reading and writing.

She would finally have her chance to learn, just like me!

## FACING MY FEARS

I worried about my safety. My parents worried, too, so they bolted our gate and locked our doors. Still, I would not let the Taliban keep me from going to school. I had a right to an education!

I woke up in a strange place.

My head and body ached.

I learned that the Taliban had shot me on the bus, and that two other girls were wounded in the attack. It was a cowardly way to silence my voice, and it did not work!

Doctors had flown me to a hospital in Birmingham, England, and saved my life.

My parents and brothers came to Birmingham as soon as they could and were so glad to see me.

The nurses brought in bags full of toys, chocolates, and teddy bears from supporters all around the world who heard what happened.

I also got thousands of letters from people who believed in my cause.

Their messages showed that I did not stand alone in my fight for girls' education.

And that I must find a way to make a difference—not only in Pakistan, but everywhere children needed help.

The injury made it hard to move my mouth.

But the doctors helped me heal so I could smile again!

## SAVE MY SEAT!

I longed to go back home to Mingora, but my parents knew it was too dangerous after the attack. Instead, I made calls to Moniba and Malka. They set aside a chair with my name on it in case I ever returned to our school.

When I left the hospital, our family had to get used to living in Birmingham.

At my new English school, the uniform was a long wool skirt and itchy blue tights.

I missed my old shalwar kamiz and all my friends.

Everyone called me the girl who got shot by the Taliban, but that's not what I wanted to be.

I wanted to be the girl who fought for peace, equality, and education.

Soon, I had another chance.

At first, my mother felt as uncomfortable in Birmingham as I did.

But she got used to our new home and began to speak out for girls' education, like my father and me!

## THINK BIG

I wanted to work for change right away, so I started the Malala Fund to guarantee every girl a free, safe, high-quality education. My prayer on the water—about helping people in need—had been answered!

On my sixteenth birthday, an important organization called the United Nations invited me to give a speech.

I stood in front of hundreds of people from all around our planet.

They listened closely to one child who spoke for millions of others.

I didn't think I could be any prouder, but I was in for a big surprise.

Everyone liked my speech, except Atal.

He wondered why people were paying so much attention to his bossy older sister!

## MY SUPERHERO OUTFIT

I chose a special shalwar kamiz for my United Nations speech, in my favorite color—pink! I also wore a white scarf that had belonged to my hero, Benazir Bhutto, the first woman to serve as Pakistan's leader. I wrapped it around my shoulders to give me courage.

At seventeen, I became the youngest person to receive the Nobel Peace Prize.

It is for people who try to make the world a better place, and I was honored for helping to improve children's lives.

When I accepted my award, I had another chance to speak about education, peace, and equal rights.

I also spoke of my home in Mingora because I missed it so much.

And can you guess what happened next?

When I was younger, I prayed to be tall.

I never grew over five feet, but at the Nobel Peace Prize ceremony, I felt as tall as the sky!

## JUST ANOTHER DAY AT SCHOOL

I learned about my Nobel Peace Prize during a high school chemistry lesson. The teachers and students celebrated with me—and then I stayed for the rest of my classes. As you know, I don't like to miss any of my time in school!

I finally went home
to Pakistan!

My heart swelled as our
family flew over Mingora
in a helicopter.

When we landed, I walked
past my old school.

I stood in my old bedroom.

And I dreamed of
what might be.

I almost never cry, even on the saddest days.

But when I saw my friends and relatives again
in Pakistan, I couldn't stop crying with joy!

## THE WARMEST WELCOME

Back home, I found that more Pakistanis than ever supported my work for girls' education. The country's leader greeted me warmly, and soldiers tipped their caps to our family. I was overjoyed to make a difference in the place I love.

I dream that you will join me in my quest.

Dear brothers and sisters, we are all one family.

Let us spread the word that every child deserves an education.

That every child deserves hope.

If we do not speak out, who will?

Together, we can change the world!

My story shows that one voice can be strong.

But millions of voices are even stronger!

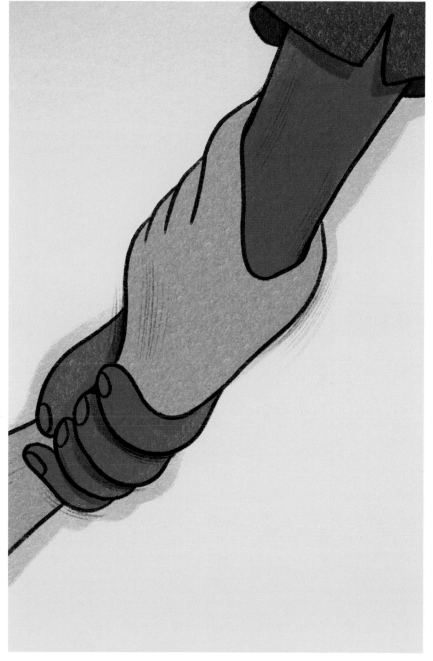

## YOU ARE A STAR

It might sound hard to change the world, but there's an easy way to start. Help just one person! Anyone can do it, including you.

# AUTHOR'S NOTE

**Malala Yousafzai** was born into a Muslim family in Pakistan's beautiful Swat Valley, speaking the Pashto language and following the traditions of her Pashtun culture.

Malala's father, Ziauddin, and mother, Tor Pekai, valued equal opportunities for girls and boys. Some in Pakistan did not, so Malala joined her father in working for change.

When Malala was ten years old, a strict religious group called the Taliban took over her town of Mingora. The Taliban used violence to deny people their freedom and even tried to keep girls from going to school. Despite the danger, Malala was determined to defend her rights.

"The Taliban could take our pens and our books, but they couldn't stop our minds from thinking," she said.

Malala spoke out for education and equality in interviews, speeches, films, and a blog. Her growing fame posed such a threat to the Taliban that they actually tried to kill her. But the attack only won her more supporters. She became one of the world's most famous activists for education.

Malala's powerful 2013 speech at the United Nations gave hope to millions of children. It also gave them the courage to stand up for their own rights.

Malala has always been a dreamer who believes that anyone—even a little girl from Mingora—can make a difference. As she said in her United Nations speech, "One child, one teacher, one book, and one pen can change the world."

## BE LIKE MALALA

- Work hard at school
- Read a lot
- Speak out against injustice
- Help people in need
- Dream big

## MALALA'S WISE WORDS

- "When the whole world is silent, even one voice becomes powerful."
- "When someone takes away your pens, you realize quite how important education is."
- "All I want is an education, and I am afraid of no one."

## WHAT MALALA LOVES ABOUT MINGORA

- The busy marketplace selling food and jewelry
- The scent of cedar and pine on the mountaintops
- Eucalyptus blossoms in spring, coating her whole town in white
- Children flying kites on streets and rooftops
- Friendly neighbors stopping by to borrow a plate of rice

## MALALA'S FAVORITE THINGS ABOUT SCHOOL

- Raising her hand to ask questions
- Learning about every subject
- Getting to know the teachers
- Making speeches in front of the class
- Laughing with friends

# MALALA'S EXCITING JOURNEY

**1997:** Born in Mingora, Pakistan; father writes her name on the family tree, defying the tradition of listing only boys' names

**2008:** Ordered to leave school by the Taliban with other girls in Mingora; makes her first major speech to Pakistani reporters, called "How Dare the Taliban Take Away My Basic Right to Education?"

**2009:** Blogs about the attack on girls for the British Broadcasting Corporation (BBC) Urdu, under the name Gul Makai; driven out of her home when the Pakistani army arrives to fight the Taliban; returns three months later

**2011:** Nominated for the International Children's Peace Prize

**2012:** Shot by a Taliban gunman, along with two of her friends, who also survive the attack; flown to Birmingham, England, for treatment; receives thousands of letters and gifts from well-wishers

**2013:** Released from the hospital; settles with her family in Birmingham; starts the Malala Fund to expand opportunities for girls; gives a powerful speech at the United Nations on her sixteenth birthday; publishes a book about her life called *I Am Malala*

**2014:** Becomes the youngest recipient of the Nobel Peace Prize

**2018:** Visits her beloved Pakistan for the first time since being shot

**2020:** Graduates from England's University of Oxford with a degree in philosophy, politics, and economics

**2021:** Marries Asser Malik in Birmingham, wearing a dress in her favorite color: pink!

# IMPORTANT TERMS

- **Activist:** A person who takes action to make the world a better place.

- **Displaced people:** Those forced to leave the place where they live, usually because of a war.

- **Equality:** People having the same rights and opportunities no matter who they are, where they come from, or what they believe.

- **Mingora:** A city on the Swat River in Pakistan with more than 300,000 people.

- **Muslim:** A follower of the Islamic religion, which is based on a holy book called the Qur'an.

- **Nobel Peace Prize:** An award presented to those who make a major contribution to world peace.

- **Pakistan:** A Muslim country in southern Asia.

- **Pashtuns:** A large ethnic group in Pakistan who speak a language called Pashto.

- **Rights:** Freedoms that all people are born with.

- **Shalwar Kamiz:** Traditional clothes worn in southern Asia. Shalwars are loose pants, wide at the waist and narrow at the bottom. A kamiz is a long shirt.

- **Taliban:** A religious and political group in Afghanistan and Pakistan that uses violence to enforce its strict beliefs.

- **United Nations:** An organization made up of countries that work together to solve the world's problems.

## RESOURCES

- Brown, Dinah. Illustrated by Andrew Thomson. *Who Is Malala Yousafzai?* New York: Penguin Workshop, 2015.

- Ellick, Adam B., dir. "Class Dismissed in Swat Valley." *New York Times*, February 22, 2009. Video, 13:32. https://www.nytimes.com/video/world/asia/1194838044017/class-dismissed-in-swat-valley.html.

- Guggenheim, Davis, dir. *He Named Me Malala*. 20th Century Fox, 2015.

- Malala Fund, "working for a world where every girl can learn and lead." https://malala.org.

- Meltzer, Brad. Illustrated by Christopher Eliopoulos. *I Am Malala Yousafzai*. New York: Dial Books for Young Readers, 2022.

- Yousafzai, Malala, with Christina Lamb. *I Am Malala: The Girl Who Stood Up for Education and Was Shot by the Taliban.* New York: Little, Brown and Company, 2013.

- Yousafzai, Malala, with Patricia McCormick. *I Am Malala: The Girl Who Stood Up for Education and Changed the World.* Young Readers Edition. New York: Little, Brown Books for Young Readers, 2014.

- Yousafzai, Malala. Illustrated by Kerascoët. *Malala's Magic Pencil.* New York: Little, Brown and Company, 2017.

- Yousafzai, Malala. "16th Birthday Speech at the United Nations." July 12, 2013. Video and transcript, 17:43. https://malala.org/newsroom/malala-un-speech.

- Yousafzai, Malala, with Liz Welch. *We Are Displaced: My Journey and Stories from Refugee Girls around the World.* New York: Little, Brown Books for Young Readers, 2019.

- Yousafzai, Ziauddin, with Louise Carpenter. *Let Her Fly: A Father's Journey.* New York: Little, Brown and Company, 2018.